REPTILE RECORD BOOK

Copyright @2018 Miles Apart Creations

All Rights Reserved

MY PETS

NAME: **TYPE:**   **AGE:**

☐ _____

☐ _____

☐ _____

☐ _____

☐ _____

REPTILE LOG – Daily Care Sheet   Date:

FEEDINGS

Pet:	Food Type:	Total:	Finished Eating:

BATHROOM / BATH TIME

Pet:	BM/Urine	Pet:	Yes/No:

NOTES: (sheds, activities, cage cleaning, etc)

Pet:	

NOTES:

REPTILE LOG – Daily Care Sheet

Date:

FEEDINGS

Pet:	Food Type:	Total:	Finished Eating:

BATHROOM / BATH TIME

Pet:	BM/Urine	Pet:	Yes/No:

NOTES: (sheds, activities, cage cleaning, etc)

Pet:	

NOTES:

REPTILE LOG – Daily Care Sheet Date:

FEEDINGS

Pet:	Food Type:	Total:	Finished Eating:

BATHROOM | BATH TIME

Pet:	BM/Urine	Pet:	Yes/No:

NOTES: (sheds, activities, cage cleaning, etc)

Pet:	

NOTES:

REPTILE LOG – Daily Care Sheet Date:

FEEDINGS

Pet:	Food Type:	Total:	Finished Eating:

BATHROOM | BATH TIME

Pet:	BM/Urine	Pet:	Yes/No:

NOTES: (sheds, activities, cage cleaning, etc)

Pet:	

NOTES:

REPTILE LOG – Daily Care Sheet   Date:

FEEDINGS

Pet:	Food Type:	Total:	Finished Eating:

BATHROOM | BATH TIME

Pet:	BM/Urine	Pet:	Yes/No:

NOTES: (sheds, activities, cage cleaning, etc)

Pet:	

NOTES:

REPTILE LOG – Daily Care Sheet Date:

FEEDINGS

Pet:	Food Type:	Total:	Finished Eating:

BATHROOM | BATH TIME

Pet:	BM/Urine	Pet:	Yes/No:

NOTES: (sheds, activities, cage cleaning, etc)

Pet:	

NOTES:

REPTILE LOG – Daily Care Sheet Date:

FEEDINGS

Pet:	Food Type:	Total:	Finished Eating:

BATHROOM | BATH TIME

Pet:	BM/Urine	Pet:	Yes/No:

NOTES: (sheds, activities, cage cleaning, etc)

Pet:	

NOTES:

REPTILE LOG – Daily Care Sheet Date:

FEEDINGS

Pet:	Food Type:	Total:	Finished Eating:

BATHROOM | BATH TIME

Pet:	BM/Urine	Pet:	Yes/No:

NOTES: (sheds, activities, cage cleaning, etc)

Pet:	

NOTES:

REPTILE LOG – Daily Care Sheet   Date:

FEEDINGS

Pet:	Food Type:	Total:	Finished Eating:

BATHROOM / BATH TIME

Pet:	BM/Urine	Pet:	Yes/No:

NOTES: (sheds, activities, cage cleaning, etc)

Pet:	

NOTES:

REPTILE LOG – Daily Care Sheet Date:

FEEDINGS

Pet:	Food Type:	Total:	Finished Eating:

BATHROOM | BATH TIME

Pet:	BM/Urine	Pet:	Yes/No:

NOTES: (sheds, activities, cage cleaning, etc)

Pet:	

NOTES:

REPTILE LOG – Daily Care Sheet   Date:

FEEDINGS

Pet:	Food Type:	Total:	Finished Eating:

BATHROOM

Pet:	BM/Urine

BATH TIME

Pet:	Yes/No:

NOTES: (sheds, activities, cage cleaning, etc)

Pet:	

NOTES:

REPTILE LOG – Daily Care Sheet Date:

FEEDINGS

Pet:	Food Type:	Total:	Finished Eating:

BATHROOM | BATH TIME

Pet:	BM/Urine	Pet:	Yes/No:

NOTES: (sheds, activities, cage cleaning, etc)

Pet:	

NOTES:

REPTILE LOG – Daily Care Sheet Date:

FEEDINGS

Pet:	Food Type:	Total:	Finished Eating:

BATHROOM / BATH TIME

Pet:	BM/Urine	Pet:	Yes/No:

NOTES: (sheds, activities, cage cleaning, etc)

Pet:	

NOTES:

REPTILE LOG – Daily Care Sheet Date:

FEEDINGS

Pet:	Food Type:	Total:	Finished Eating:

BATHROOM | BATH TIME

Pet:	BM/Urine	Pet:	Yes/No:

NOTES: (sheds, activities, cage cleaning, etc)

Pet:	

NOTES:

REPTILE LOG – Daily Care Sheet   Date:

FEEDINGS

Pet:	Food Type:	Total:	Finished Eating:

BATHROOM / BATH TIME

Pet:	BM/Urine	Pet:	Yes/No:

NOTES: (sheds, activities, cage cleaning, etc)

Pet:	

NOTES:

REPTILE LOG – Daily Care Sheet Date:

FEEDINGS

Pet:	Food Type:	Total:	Finished Eating:

BATHROOM | BATH TIME

Pet:	BM/Urine	Pet:	Yes/No:

NOTES: (sheds, activities, cage cleaning, etc)

Pet:	

NOTES:

REPTILE LOG – Daily Care Sheet

Date:

FEEDINGS

Pet:	Food Type:	Total:	Finished Eating:

BATHROOM | BATH TIME

Pet:	BM/Urine	Pet:	Yes/No:

NOTES: (sheds, activities, cage cleaning, etc)

Pet:	

NOTES:

REPTILE LOG – Daily Care Sheet

Date:

FEEDINGS

Pet:	Food Type:	Total:	Finished Eating:

BATHROOM | BATH TIME

Pet:	BM/Urine	Pet:	Yes/No:

NOTES: (sheds, activities, cage cleaning, etc)

Pet:	

NOTES:

REPTILE LOG – Daily Care Sheet

Date:

FEEDINGS

Pet:	Food Type:	Total:	Finished Eating:

BATHROOM | BATH TIME

Pet:	BM/Urine	Pet:	Yes/No:

NOTES: (sheds, activities, cage cleaning, etc)

Pet:	

NOTES:

REPTILE LOG – Daily Care Sheet Date:

FEEDINGS

Pet:	Food Type:	Total:	Finished Eating:

BATHROOM | BATH TIME

Pet:	BM/Urine	Pet:	Yes/No:

NOTES: (sheds, activities, cage cleaning, etc)

Pet:	

NOTES:

REPTILE LOG – Daily Care Sheet

Date:

FEEDINGS

Pet:	Food Type:	Total:	Finished Eating:

BATHROOM / BATH TIME

Pet:	BM/Urine	Pet:	Yes/No:

NOTES: (sheds, activities, cage cleaning, etc)

Pet:	

NOTES:

REPTILE LOG – Daily Care Sheet   Date:

FEEDINGS

Pet:	Food Type:	Total:	Finished Eating:

BATHROOM / BATH TIME

Pet:	BM/Urine	Pet:	Yes/No:

NOTES: (sheds, activities, cage cleaning, etc)

Pet:	

NOTES:

REPTILE LOG – Daily Care Sheet   Date:

FEEDINGS

Pet:	Food Type:	Total:	Finished Eating:

BATHROOM | BATH TIME

Pet:	BM/Urine	Pet:	Yes/No:

NOTES: (sheds, activities, cage cleaning, etc)

Pet:	

NOTES:

REPTILE LOG – Daily Care Sheet   Date:

FEEDINGS

Pet:	Food Type:	Total:	Finished Eating:

BATHROOM | | BATH TIME | |

Pet:	BM/Urine	Pet:	Yes/No:

NOTES: (sheds, activities, cage cleaning, etc)

Pet:	

NOTES:

REPTILE LOG – Daily Care Sheet Date:

FEEDINGS

Pet:	Food Type:	Total:	Finished Eating:

BATHROOM | BATH TIME

Pet:	BM/Urine	Pet:	Yes/No:

NOTES: (sheds, activities, cage cleaning, etc)

Pet:	

NOTES:

REPTILE LOG – Daily Care Sheet Date:

FEEDINGS

Pet:	Food Type:	Total:	Finished Eating:

BATHROOM | BATH TIME

Pet:	BM/Urine	Pet:	Yes/No:

NOTES: (sheds, activities, cage cleaning, etc)

Pet:	

NOTES:

REPTILE LOG – Daily Care Sheet

Date:

FEEDINGS

Pet:	Food Type:	Total:	Finished Eating:

BATHROOM

Pet:	BM/Urine

BATH TIME

Pet:	Yes/No:

NOTES: (sheds, activities, cage cleaning, etc)

Pet:	

NOTES:

REPTILE LOG – Daily Care Sheet

Date:

FEEDINGS

Pet:	Food Type:	Total:	Finished Eating:

BATHROOM | BATH TIME

Pet:	BM/Urine	Pet:	Yes/No:

NOTES: (sheds, activities, cage cleaning, etc)

Pet:	

NOTES:

REPTILE LOG – Daily Care Sheet

Date:

FEEDINGS

Pet:	Food Type:	Total:	Finished Eating:

BATHROOM | BATH TIME

Pet:	BM/Urine	Pet:	Yes/No:

NOTES: (sheds, activities, cage cleaning, etc)

Pet:	

NOTES:

REPTILE LOG – Daily Care Sheet   Date:

FEEDINGS

Pet:	Food Type:	Total:	Finished Eating:

BATHROOM | BATH TIME

Pet:	BM/Urine	Pet:	Yes/No:

NOTES: (sheds, activities, cage cleaning, etc)

Pet:	

NOTES:

REPTILE LOG – Daily Care Sheet

Date:

FEEDINGS

Pet:	Food Type:	Total:	Finished Eating:

BATHROOM | BATH TIME

Pet:	BM/Urine	Pet:	Yes/No:

NOTES: (sheds, activities, cage cleaning, etc)

Pet:	

NOTES:

REPTILE LOG – Daily Care Sheet

Date:

FEEDINGS

Pet:	Food Type:	Total:	Finished Eating:

BATHROOM | BATH TIME

Pet:	BM/Urine	Pet:	Yes/No:

NOTES: (sheds, activities, cage cleaning, etc)

Pet:	

NOTES:

REPTILE LOG – Daily Care Sheet   Date:

FEEDINGS

Pet:	Food Type:	Total:	Finished Eating:

BATHROOM / BATH TIME

BATHROOM		BATH TIME	
Pet:	BM/Urine	Pet:	Yes/No:

NOTES: (sheds, activities, cage cleaning, etc)

Pet:	

NOTES:

REPTILE LOG – Daily Care Sheet

Date:

FEEDINGS

Pet:	Food Type:	Total:	Finished Eating:

BATHROOM

Pet:	BM/Urine

BATH TIME

Pet:	Yes/No:

NOTES: (sheds, activities, cage cleaning, etc)

Pet:	

NOTES:

REPTILE LOG – Daily Care Sheet

Date:

FEEDINGS

Pet:	Food Type:	Total:	Finished Eating:

BATHROOM | BATH TIME

Pet:	BM/Urine	Pet:	Yes/No:

NOTES: (sheds, activities, cage cleaning, etc)

Pet:	

NOTES:

REPTILE LOG – Daily Care Sheet Date:

FEEDINGS

Pet:	Food Type:	Total:	Finished Eating:

BATHROOM | BATH TIME

Pet:	BM/Urine	Pet:	Yes/No:

NOTES: (sheds, activities, cage cleaning, etc)

Pet:	

NOTES:

REPTILE LOG – Daily Care Sheet   Date:

FEEDINGS

Pet:	Food Type:	Total:	Finished Eating:

BATHROOM / BATH TIME

Pet:	BM/Urine	Pet:	Yes/No:

NOTES: (sheds, activities, cage cleaning, etc)

Pet:	

NOTES:

REPTILE LOG – Daily Care Sheet

Date:

FEEDINGS

Pet:	Food Type:	Total:	Finished Eating:

BATHROOM | BATH TIME

Pet:	BM/Urine	Pet:	Yes/No:

NOTES: (sheds, activities, cage cleaning, etc)

Pet:	

NOTES:

REPTILE LOG – Daily Care Sheet

Date:

FEEDINGS

Pet:	Food Type:	Total:	Finished Eating:

BATHROOM / BATH TIME

Pet:	BM/Urine	Pet:	Yes/No:

NOTES: (sheds, activities, cage cleaning, etc)

Pet:	

NOTES:

REPTILE LOG – Daily Care Sheet Date:

FEEDINGS

Pet:	Food Type:	Total:	Finished Eating:

BATHROOM | BATH TIME

Pet:	BM/Urine	Pet:	Yes/No:

NOTES: (sheds, activities, cage cleaning, etc)

Pet:	

NOTES:

REPTILE LOG – Daily Care Sheet   Date:

FEEDINGS

Pet:	Food Type:	Total:	Finished Eating:

BATHROOM / BATH TIME

Pet:	BM/Urine	Pet:	Yes/No:

NOTES: (sheds, activities, cage cleaning, etc)

Pet:	

NOTES:

REPTILE LOG – Daily Care Sheet Date:

FEEDINGS

Pet:	Food Type:	Total:	Finished Eating:

BATHROOM | BATH TIME

Pet:	BM/Urine	Pet:	Yes/No:

NOTES: (sheds, activities, cage cleaning, etc)

Pet:	

NOTES:

REPTILE LOG – Daily Care Sheet

Date:

FEEDINGS

Pet:	Food Type:	Total:	Finished Eating:

BATHROOM | BATH TIME

Pet:	BM/Urine	Pet:	Yes/No:

NOTES: (sheds, activities, cage cleaning, etc)

Pet:	

NOTES:

REPTILE LOG – Daily Care Sheet Date:

FEEDINGS

Pet:	Food Type:	Total:	Finished Eating:

BATHROOM | BATH TIME

Pet:	BM/Urine	Pet:	Yes/No:

NOTES: (sheds, activities, cage cleaning, etc)

Pet:	

NOTES:

REPTILE LOG - Daily Care Sheet

Date:

FEEDINGS

Pet:	Food Type:	Total:	Finished Eating:

BATHROOM | BATH TIME

Pet:	BM/Urine	Pet:	Yes/No:

NOTES: (sheds, activities, cage cleaning, etc)

Pet:	

NOTES:

REPTILE LOG – Daily Care Sheet   Date:

FEEDINGS

Pet:	Food Type:	Total:	Finished Eating:

BATHROOM | BATH TIME

Pet:	BM/Urine	Pet:	Yes/No:

NOTES: (sheds, activities, cage cleaning, etc)

Pet:	

NOTES:

REPTILE LOG – Daily Care Sheet

Date:

FEEDINGS

Pet:	Food Type:	Total:	Finished Eating:

BATHROOM | BATH TIME

Pet:	BM/Urine	Pet:	Yes/No:

NOTES: (sheds, activities, cage cleaning, etc)

Pet:	

NOTES:

REPTILE LOG – Daily Care Sheet

Date:

FEEDINGS

Pet:	Food Type:	Total:	Finished Eating:

BATHROOM | BATH TIME

Pet:	BM/Urine	Pet:	Yes/No:

NOTES: (sheds, activities, cage cleaning, etc)

Pet:	

NOTES:

REPTILE LOG – Daily Care Sheet   Date:

FEEDINGS

Pet:	Food Type:	Total:	Finished Eating:

BATHROOM

Pet:	BM/Urine

BATH TIME

Pet:	Yes/No:

NOTES: (sheds, activities, cage cleaning, etc)

Pet:	

NOTES:

REPTILE LOG – Daily Care Sheet   Date:

FEEDINGS

Pet:	Food Type:	Total:	Finished Eating:

BATHROOM | BATH TIME

Pet:	BM/Urine	Pet:	Yes/No:

NOTES: (sheds, activities, cage cleaning, etc)

Pet:	

NOTES:

REPTILE LOG – Daily Care Sheet

Date:

FEEDINGS

Pet:	Food Type:	Total:	Finished Eating:

BATHROOM | BATH TIME

Pet:	BM/Urine	Pet:	Yes/No:

NOTES: (sheds, activities, cage cleaning, etc)

Pet:	

NOTES:

REPTILE LOG – Daily Care Sheet   Date:

FEEDINGS

Pet:	Food Type:	Total:	Finished Eating:

BATHROOM | BATH TIME

Pet:	BM/Urine	Pet:	Yes/No:

NOTES: (sheds, activities, cage cleaning, etc)

Pet:	

NOTES:

REPTILE LOG – Daily Care Sheet Date:

FEEDINGS

Pet:	Food Type:	Total:	Finished Eating:

BATHROOM | BATH TIME

Pet:	BM/Urine	Pet:	Yes/No:

NOTES: (sheds, activities, cage cleaning, etc)

Pet:	

NOTES:

REPTILE LOG – Daily Care Sheet

Date:

FEEDINGS

Pet:	Food Type:	Total:	Finished Eating:

BATHROOM | BATH TIME

Pet:	BM/Urine	Pet:	Yes/No:

NOTES: (sheds, activities, cage cleaning, etc)

Pet:	

NOTES:

REPTILE LOG – Daily Care Sheet Date:

FEEDINGS

Pet:	Food Type:	Total:	Finished Eating:

BATHROOM | BATH TIME

Pet:	BM/Urine	Pet:	Yes/No:

NOTES: (sheds, activities, cage cleaning, etc)

Pet:	

NOTES:

REPTILE LOG – Daily Care Sheet   Date:

FEEDINGS

Pet:	Food Type:	Total:	Finished Eating:

BATHROOM | BATH TIME

Pet:	BM/Urine	Pet:	Yes/No:

NOTES: (sheds, activities, cage cleaning, etc)

Pet:	

NOTES:

REPTILE LOG – Daily Care Sheet

Date:

FEEDINGS

Pet:	Food Type:	Total:	Finished Eating:

BATHROOM

Pet:	BM/Urine

BATH TIME

Pet:	Yes/No:

NOTES: (sheds, activities, cage cleaning, etc)

Pet:	

NOTES:

REPTILE LOG – Daily Care Sheet

Date:

FEEDINGS

Pet:	Food Type:	Total:	Finished Eating:

BATHROOM / BATH TIME

Pet:	BM/Urine	Pet:	Yes/No:

NOTES: (sheds, activities, cage cleaning, etc)

Pet:	

NOTES:

NOTES:

NOTES:

Made in the USA
Las Vegas, NV
10 October 2021